Living Senselessly on the Grid

Living Senselessly on the Grid

Table of Contents

Foreword

Living off the grip became a highly popular choice to those people who wish to affirm their sovereignty and to escape from their dependence to fossil fuels when it comes to energy supply. To have this kind of way of life must be a very useful idea if you are aiming to reduce your monthly bills and to show your overflowing concern to Mother Earth.

This book will serve as your guide in obtaining success as you start to live off the grid. Find the answers to all questions you have in mind. So, start reading now and have fun!

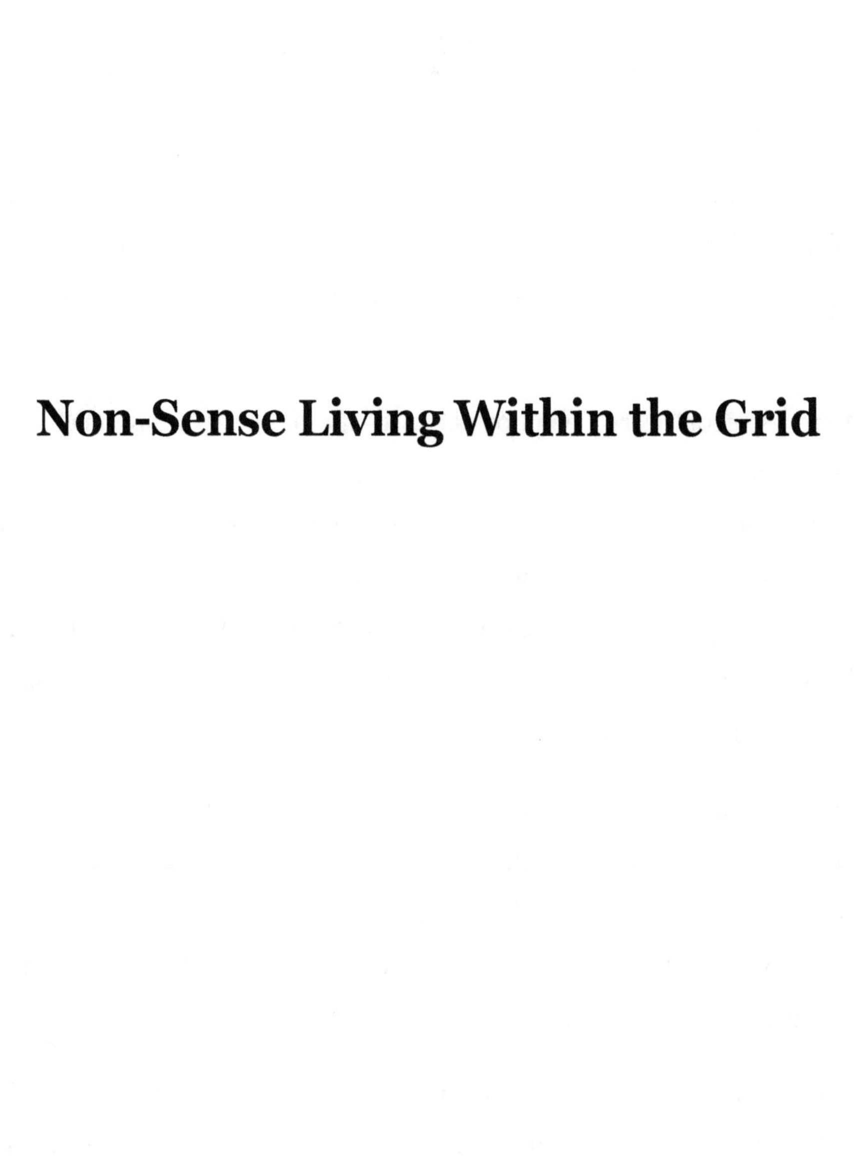

Non-Sense Living Within the Grid

Chapter 1:

Living off the Grid Basics

When you hear the term "living off the road", what does it means? Living off the grid doesn't mean you have to live in a way the hermit does. The truth is most people who choose to live in this way are actually somewhat sociable.

When a person hears "living off the grid", he or she typically imagines a kind of life in a far-flung area. A person imagines his or her self living in a farm where there are no utilities like electricity. Though some people choose to live in that way, the true meaning of living off the grid is not to depend completely on the usual source of energy that power grids offer. You will be able to get nearer to a 100% when you search for an alternative system to use in generating electricity.

There are various reasons why a person can live off the grid but, usually, off-grid solar electric systems are used in the remote areas where connecting to a local utility grid can't be possible or it is prohibitively costly. These systems are also suitable for those areas wherein grid power is incompatible or it can be because of the demand of a self-sufficient lifestyle.

Whatever your reason for choosing to live off the grid, you should consider first what you will need. The following are the things you require to start the off the grid life:

12 Things You Have to Go Off the Grid

- Money – living off the grid will not be easy for you to do if you do not have money inside your pocket. With money, you can buy things you need so that you can live off the grid. Cash is very important especially if you will live off the grid with your family. The truth is to do anything today requires money and typically, you need lots of it.

- Land – when it comes to living off the grid, first and foremost, you need to look for a place to go. In choosing a place where you can live off the grid, you must choose one with adequate supply of water. Always take into account that you'll be off the grid. Meaning, you would be producing your own electricity by using solar and wind energy. In selecting the best location to live off the grid, you should look for a place that has good sun and moderate wind. It must be located close to other resources so that you will be living off the grid in a safe, manageable and comfortable way.

- When you have children, you should consider your location in relationship to hospitals, schools, shopping stores and entertainment centers. If you already have your family, you should never forget to consider the needs of your husband or wife as well.

- Shelter – you also need to have a shelter. Once again, you have to choose one that is safe, energy-efficient, comfortable and affordable. Cabins and homes are known to be the most affordable choices and they are also the most attractive ones to most individuals. Converted buses, RVs, and the like are also available.

- Water – if you are planning to buy land, you should look for one that offers a sufficient supply of water. For sure, there are lots of choices to choose from. It is best to see and check them one by one before making a choice.

- Food – don't forget to include foods in your list of necessities when living off the grid. Most people who prefer to live off the grid grow their own foods. There are various foods that are highly suitable for off the grid way of life.

- Livestock – these include chickens, cows and pigs which are known to be the best sources of meat. These meats are rich in protein and you don't have to harvest them.

- Energy - of course, when you choose to live off the grid, you will need to have your own source of power. This is where you should consider the use of solar or wind power. If you live off the grid, hopefully, you will not be using more energy. But, actually, the amount of energy you consume every day does not matter because you will be supplying your home with electricity using your own solar or wind power system. With an off the grid system, a tiny wind turbine, solar panels, a micro-hydro system or an amalgamation of the mentioned technologies are used to supply adequate supply of power. In certain off-grid systems, a home-based backup generator might be included as well and it is used to supply power if the renewable technologies are incapable of producing a sufficient supply to suit the needs. Off-grid living relieves completely your dependency on electrical utility and that is because this system offers you enough supply of power. For this reason, off-grid systems are usually bigger compared to grid-ties. To become fully independent, the system you use should have a bigger wind generator or a series of solar panels then paired it with a greater storage capacity of the battery. When you are able to do it successfully, you will find living off the grid helps you save thousands of cash.

- Septic – you are responsible for your waste whether you choose to live off the grid or not. Having a septic system can be a good choice.

- Cuttings and Seeds – to grow foods, you should have some seeds to start building your garden. These are quite cheap.

- Materials – there are some tools that you need to use when living off the grid and these are the bolts and nuts, lumber, screw, metal, wire, cable, hoses, fencing, rope and many more. These are the things you should use in building and completing the repairs required in your off the grid homestead.

- Tools and Equipment – if you will be building your off the grid cabin by using the materials available on your area, you'll require many tools and equipment. Examples of these are hammer, screwdrivers, wrenches, drill, circular saw, lawnmower or tractor and many more.

- Commitment – you almost have all but your off the grid life will never be complete without commitment. You need to be committed and sincere to meet your goal for choosing to live in this way or else all your efforts will be wasted.

All of these things should be considered and prepared before you start your attempt to make a big change in your life. Always keep in mind that without these things, it will be too impossible for you to achieve your goal – to become fully independent.

Chapter 2:

Having the Right Mindset

As you pursue to live off the grid, one thing that you should consider is to develop the right mindset. The spirit of sovereignty and dedication to attain a sustainable way of life is essential to obtain success as you go and choose off-grid living. But, you will not escape from the society completely as even the self-sufficient people are obliged to pay the property taxes.

Living off the grid means various things to various people. Some persons desire modern conveniences & huge power-generating stations. Meanwhile, other people are happier in taking one step back & living with bucolic types of food storage and heating. Going off-grid could be a pricey proposition when you try to replace the modern amenities you have today.

To develop the right mindset, you should weigh all things and make sure that you are fully prepared to live in this way. Pay attention to every aspect that must be taken into account. Look at the benefits that you can obtain from living off the grid. You should have a particular reason why you choose to practice this way of life. Use that reason as your motivation tool to achieve success.

So now, can you imagine yourself living in off-grid style? If you are really serious about it, start focusing your attention to your goal to have the right mindset!

Chapter 3:

Finding the Right Place to Live

Living off the grid means you build a home in a place where you would not depend on the utilities available in your community. Instead, the off-grid homes use different mechanisms to become independent. Some persons use the phrase "off the grid" when pertaining to living away from the governmental organizations. But, in any case, the initial step to take is to find a location for a house that has the ability to sustain itself with no reliance on external assistance.

Finding the right place to live if you choose to live off the grid may not be an easy thing to do. But, you can get a lot of help from following these steps:

1. Find a location that is situated far from the major cities. Trying to live off the grid inside a busy city is impossible. So try to find a place where you can truly feel that everything will be easy.

2. Look for a land that is huge and sufficient for your needs. When you require a big deal of firewood, ensure that you have a wide land where you can get what you need. When it comes to farming, you can grow a big garden or if maintaining farm animals is a part of your whole plan, make sure that you have purchased enough territory for it.

3. You can shop for a residential property which comes with some pieces of the important water equipment you require to live off the grid. It means that you have to search for a property with a well that is in good condition. If you will be able to find a house with installed septic

system, you are a one step closer to achieve comfortable off-grid lifestyle as well.

4. Look for the property with independent source of power. For example, you may search for a house with wind, solar, or geothermal system that is already installed. Instead, when you find a certain location where building a house with good south front exposure to install your solar power system, you can integrate power support while time goes on.

5. Select a final location with food sources & emergency services inside an accessible space, especially when you're not planning to grow ample supply of food to be fully independent on your own property. Solitude and disconnection are commonly preferred by most people who choose to live off the grid but safety must be a concern as well.

To find the right place where you can truly live off the grid, you should be careful and practical in choosing. Follow these tips to avoid difficulties in selecting the best place to stay to have a comfortable off-grid lifestyle.

Chapter 4:

Solar Energy

Solar energy is among the most desirable and ecologically sound sources of electricity today. This form of power has been known and used by people for the past several years. It is used by plant, microbial & animal life as the basic supply of energy.

Fossil fuels, the recognized main source of energy in today's generation, are created from animals and plants that existed in the world a long time ago. Only today is when humans were able to capture solar power to make it available anytime whether day or night.

People who choose to live off the grid should consider the use of solar energy instead of the fossil fuels. Solar power does not emit carbon dioxide and other forms of dangerous toxins that threaten the environment. Likewise, solar energy is obtained and gathered by almost each single type of life.

Solar power has been considered as a highly essential alternative source of power that can help people in taking care of the environment. It could also help in cutting down people's dependence on the effective but harmful source of power – fossil fuels. Most people think that solar energy is expensive and they are definitely wrong. It won't cause you more if you will choose to live off the grid just like what other homeowners do.

If your house will be supplied with energy by a solar panel system, it may cost you over $30,000. But, the cost will definitely go down due to some factors such as tax credits, grants and rebates that will pull down the price of solar panel system installation by thirty percent or more.

Depending on your needs, you can choose between the sizes available when it comes to solar panel systems. To make sure that your budget will just be enough to meet your needs; you can opt to a smaller solar power system. Just make sure that the energy it can produce will just be enough for your household energy needs. It will cost you less while it helps in reducing your current electric bill. Besides, this will certainly make your house more environmentally sound.

As of now, fossil fuels are used in generating electricity and it is the practice in most countries all over the world. Hence, minimizing your use of electrical energy from an area power firm by fifty percent is actually a very crucial action to be taken towards establishing a sustainable energy grid.

Chapter 5:

Wind Energy

Wind energy is among the most well-known sources of alternative energy in the present years. This is also known as the fastest growing power source within the industry. More people realized the major benefits of applying this form of energy and that is why the installation of wind turbines increased significantly in the previous few years.

With this form of renewable power source, the wind that blows freely will turn the wind turbines which are positioned strategically that will produce electricity. If the wind speeds are stronger, the wind turbines would produce greater power. Inside of those areas that may produce powerful wind speeds, choosing to use this kind of energy as the alternative source of energy to supply power to homes and businesses will be the smart option.

Since the time when people became aware of the negative effects of fossil fuels to the environment, the need for alternative energy sources have increased. Wind and solar power are considered as the most commonly used energy sources considering that they are both renewable and won't cause danger to the environment. Both of these sources of renewable energy have the potential to be the primary source of power which can replace the fossil fuels eventually.

The use of this energy for household use comes with a lot of advantages which can be somewhat enticing for most homeowners. This is true especially to those people who are facing problems with their electric monthly bills.

Though having wind generators or wind turbines installed in your home can help you save money, you can be sure that there's a high amount of return in your investment. And, you will obtain that someday. Always take into account that wind is available always and it is for free so what you need is to spend some money on the initial cost and for the maintenance cost for some time.

The best thing to know about it is that the wind generators have more capacity to provide a sufficient supply of power to a house. Can you imagine how big you can save on your electric bills each month alone? Depending on how much electricity you consume in each day of your life, living off the grid is certainly possible with the help of wind power.

There are some benefits that you can get when you switch to the application of wind power as the main source of electricity for your home. First of all, it has something to do with the decrease in the usual amount of your monthly electric bills. As you live off the grid, a wind turbine generator could help you reduce your monthly payments particularly on your electric bills.

The next benefit is the remarkable reduction of energy outages. As the electricity produced and supplied by your wind turbine generators is kept in the battery banks, you'll always have extra supply of electricity that you can use when something bad happens to your home power grid. The last one is the truth that wind energy is friendly to the environment.

If you're worried about your carbon footprint, you don't have to feel that way anymore. Wind energy is clean just like the water. It doesn't produce gases which can cause harm to the environment so wind power will be truly helpful especially today when air pollution became the main concern of most environmentalists. So if you want to live off the grid, you should switch to wind power; it's an excellent choice for you!

Chapter 6:

Water collection Systems

A place with stable water supply is important to off the grid way of life. A drilled well is typical and it requires the usage of the pump and a huge collection tank designed for water storage. A well is typically used for supplying clean and potable water and it must be treated and tested on a regular basis and when needed in order to ensure that the water is safe for consumption.

The rain barrels could supplement the supply of water especially when it comes to gardening needs or depending on the annual rainfall within your location, providing more water for household purposes. Collecting and storing water from a stream located close to your location sounds simple yet the possibility of contamination from animal waste, bacteria & other pollutants necessitates the application of water filtration & purification systems that may require extra solar energy units to work.

Chapter 7:

Waste Disposal

You should dispose your waste properly and that's a fact of life. In terms of human waste, some homeowners prefer to use a composting lavatory system. On the other hand, this system may not be legal at some point depending on the ordinance or zoning limitations and regulations enforcement inside the county where your property is situated.

Waste disposal is among the most crucial considerations in establishing a homestead within a far-flung area. Bathroom facilities are usually one of the first facilities to be built. There are various solutions that are highly appropriate for homesteaders and residents of the isolated rural locations with no instant access to sewer or water systems. These solutions are also suitable for those people who are trying to live off the grid and for anyone who is concerned with minimizing their effect on the environment. There are two forms of waste disposal systems and these are the composting and toilets and outhouses.

Aside from these, living off the grid also involves the issues regarding material garbage. In dealing with them, you may follow this simple and straightforward five step process:

1. Sort – when the grid went down & you know that it'll last for a week or longer than that, few of your habits when it comes to trash disposal may need changes. The initial step that you should take is to start segregating the trash into 4 groups namely: those that will biodegrade instantly, paper products, metals and plastics and; sanitary items.

2. Dump – for the biodegradable materials, it can be deposited into a container or pile that is located at a distance from your home. These materials will start to compost and you can use them later for your garden.

3. Drain – following the initial sorting process, you have to drain off the liquids that are still inside the containers. For the non-fat containing fluids, you can simply pour them on the soil. For fatty oils and liquids, you may pour them on a small cat-hole dug and then cover that with dirt from the tunnel. It will help in preventing the attraction of insects and animals. Don't forget that it isn't ideal to mix oils and fats to a compost heap you've made from the "dump" step because it can affect and stop the process of composting.

4. Burn – there are some garbage that you can burn such as paper products and when you have spare time for them, you will realize that most paper products such as newspaper and junk mail could be made into useful paper logs. These will be good fuel sources that you will need for cooking or heating once the grid stops working.

5. Bury – for the other garbage such as plastics, metal and sanitary products, you can store them for a long time as long as you could double up the trash bags which are placed in a container with cover. But, when the grid will be down for a long time, the last resort you have is to bury these waste materials. You can dig a pit or trench which is deep enough. That way, at least a 1 ½ feet of compacted dirt can cover the garbage well. Likewise, ensure that the pit is at least a hundred feet apart from the water source.

Chapter 8:

Food Source

As you set up your off from the grid homestead, you will also need to consider other important things to your day-to-day living and one of them is food.

Most people who choose to live off from the ground prefer to grow and harvest their own foods which are usually vegetables and fruits. Indeed, you will need to spend more time in growing your food and the quickest crops would grow in just a few weeks to one month. Usually, 30 days is long enough to go without food. Hence, you have to come up with a way of how you will be able to survive for at least during the first thirty to sixty days.

So what you're going to consume within 90 days? It is where dry foods and livestock come in. Dry foods like beans, rice, oats and the like are good beginning point while preserved canned goods such as jams, veggies, jellies, smoked meats and dried fruits would last for a while. These goods will give a sufficient supply of foods to eat during your first few months on your homestead.

Livestock like chickens, cows and pigs are known to be good sources of food. The meat gives protein, and you don't have to harvest it until you can eat it. The only problem is you have to preserve the leftover meat that will require electricity when you need to freeze it.

Here are certain ideas that you may consider when it comes to livestock:

- Turkeys

- Chickens

- Ducks

- Pheasant

- Geese

- Pigs

- Cows

- Rabbits and;

- Fish

Chapter 9:

What to Avoid

As you choose to live off the grid, there are some things you have to avoid and there are things you need to keep in mind at all times. So what those things are? Hey they are:

What to Avoid If You Like to Live off the Grid

- You can escape from your woes by living out of the grid. It is not a good idea so you must avoid thinking of it. You must not forget that moving off the grid is not an escape hatch for your personal and financial woes. So if you are planning to go somewhere and your reason for choosing to live in this way is like this, you should stop. Living an independent life doesn't excuses and spares you from any debt you have accumulated. The same thing goes with any problem that you've caused in your life today.

- Living off the grid will spare you from your obligations in life. Don't think of living off the grid as a way to avoid your responsibilities in life. Whether you live in a remote area or not, still, you are solely responsible for your obligations. You still need to provide the needs of your family especially your children. The responsibilities you used to have will still be your obligations to fulfill even when you live off the grid.

- Living off the grid is about being self-sufficient. You will never be self-reliant when you have responsibilities that are attached to you. Don't forget that hiding off the grid will not eliminate your previous debit. Knowing this, will you still desire to make a change in your life?

- Leave and start living off the grid without a plan. Before you leave, see to it that everything is fine. How will you be able to live independently if you don't have all the things you require? It is not bad to start changing your life today but be sure that you are prepared enough to do it. Since you already know the things you need in living off the grid, focus your attention on them for now and don't rush.

- Break the conditions if you don't have a choice at all. If you are a person who have this kind of philosophy in life then living off the grid is not for you. To live off grid comes with certain rules that one must follow like overcoming your dependence on the usual source of energy that power grids offer. It is very important to take those conditions seriously. Remember, your goal here is to be self-sufficient and you will not be able to achieve that if you will break the rules.

- Pursue your off the grid lifestyle though your finances are already in trouble. You should not sacrifice the other aspects of your life just to attain your dream. When your finances are already in trouble and you are still eager to continue what you have started yet you're sensing no practicable way to do so within the time frame, you must consult and seek help from a professional financial planner. Or, you can set a schedule to meet a credit counselor.

- Spending your resources carelessly. You have nothing to turn to when you choose to live off the grid. As said before, you will live on your own and you can only use your own resources to suit your needs. How will you be able to make your resources sufficient for your everyday requirements if you will be careless in using them? This is one of the common mistakes that a person makes while living out of the grid. One typical scenario that you can associate to this is the impractical use of the energy produced by your own power generating system. This will cost you more so you end up thinking of living out of the grid as an expensive choice.

These things will hinder you from achieving your purpose of living off the grid. So, it is very important to avoid them. You should follow these tips conscientiously.

Chapter 10:

The Benefits of Living Off the Grid

Everything you have done as you choose to live off the grid will be paid in the end. This way of life comes with challenges but it also has lots of benefits that will really make you happy and proud of yourself once you are able to achieve success. Before you learn the benefits of living off the grid, you should focus first on the top reasons why you must prefer to spend your life in this way. These reasons will motivate you to do whatever it takes just to reap the advantages in the end.

The Top 10 Reasons to Live Off the Grid

- To become more aware of the environment

- To have a more independent lifestyle not only for yourself but for your loved ones as well

- To feel security as you are far from the concerns associate with the busy city

- To learn how to become the master of your own fate

- To obtain a simple and more satisfying way of life

- To learn how to produce your own foods

- To achieve a kind of life that is totally free from debt and learn how to be prudent

- To understand that regardless of what may happen to the world, your own family is ready

- To learn how you will be able to live off the land

- To become an example to your children and giving them a bequest of independence

When you follow these reasons with all of your heart, you will meet success and you will attain the benefits of off the grid way of life. These advantages are the following:

- Reduced cost of energy – when you prefer to spend your life in this way, the cost of your monthly electrical bill will drop significantly. The truth is, in some instances, the electric company might even cut you a check.

- Freedom from being dependent to utility grid. You will not have constant reliance on the utility grid. Other people believe that the grid will never be available forever. It will never happen and that is true.

- Reduced risk of climate-related incidence of power loss – if the weather becomes funky, power may still be available. But, when a powerful storm hits your location, the power grid will be affected and it will lose its capacity to produce and provide power. That's the right time to use the alternative sources of energy.

- Lots of home design choices – most designs of houses today could be off the grid. While these homes are typically smaller, it will not be the case at all times. Off the grid way of living is not simply a something that folks in this planet do. Though, these home styles are energy-efficient and excellent choices so you may desire to look into them.

- Increased knowledge about the environment. You'll get a completely new education when you choose living off the grid. Managing the alternative power systems, living in a simpler way and learning the most effective ways to save provide a hands-on education which you will never get wholly from the books. Most of the off the grid homestead dwellers think of this way of life as a life choice and not as a way their house is designed.

- Reduced carbon footprint – your carbon footprint will be diminished once you live off the grid. You can determine how much your carbon footprint is by using a carbon footprint calculating tool.

So now that you have learned everything about living off the grid, are you ready enough to face the challenge? If you are 100% sure then take it! Good luck!